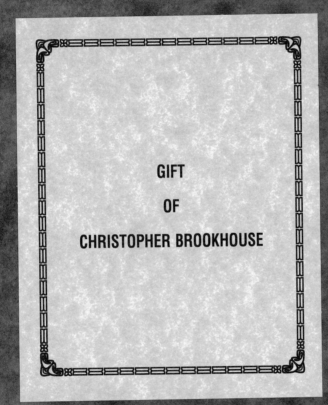

ELYSIUM

a gathering of souls

E L Y

S I U M

a gathering of souls

NEW ORLEANS CEMETERIES

PHOTOGRAPHS BY

SANDRA RUSSELL CLARK

WITH A FOREWORD BY

ANDREI CODRESCU

AND AN INTRODUCTION BY

PATRICIA BRADY

Louisiana State University Press / *Baton Rouge and London*

#36783835

06 05 04 03 02 01 00 99 98 97   5 4 3 2 1

Designer: *Amanda McDonald Key*

Display typeface: *Mason and Snell Roundhand*

Text typeface: *Sabon*

Printer and binder: Sung In Printing America, Inc.

LIBRARY OF CONGRESS CATALOGING-IN-PUBLICATION DATA

Clark, Sandra Russell.

    Elysium—a gathering of souls : New Orleans cemeteries /

photographs by Sandra Russell Clark ; with a foreword by Andrei

Codrescu and an introduction by Patricia Brady.

      p.   cm.

    ISBN 0-8071-2228-9 (cloth : alk. paper)

    1. Cemeteries—Louisiana—New Orleans—Pictorial works. 2.

New Orleans (La.)—Pictorial works.

F379.N562A2   1997

976.3' 35—dc21   97-16235

                                      CIP

This project is supported by a grant from the Louisiana Endowment for the

Humanities, a state affiliate of the National Endowment for the Humani-

ties.

The paper in this book meets the guidelines for permanence and durability

of the Committee on Production Guidelines for Book Longevity of the

Council on Library Resources. ♾

In loving memory of Albertine and Sylvia

The nihilists say it is the end;

the fundamentalists, the beginning;

when in reality it is no more than

a single tenant or family moving

out of a tenement or a town.

—William Faulkner

Contents

A Trumpet in Heaven

SOME NOTES ON THE DISPOSITION OF BODIES IN NEW ORLEANS AND THE STORIES THEY TELL

Andrei Codrescu

CEMETERIES are reassuring: they provide continuity. The dearly departed do not need as much room as they used to, but they still have an address. They are available 365 days a year, twenty-four hours a day in any weather. The fog may be draping their little house or a downpour trying to drown it, but invariably the occupants are at home. This may be small comfort to the widow who could never keep the living husband home, but it is a promissory note that things will be different in heaven. Catholic tombs are waiting rooms for the Day of Judgment. The dead, in their perennial little houses, rehearse the defense they will offer the Almighty and rest for the day when they will be called to rise and exert their creaky bodies again. The cities of the dead are busy places, but like cities of the living, they vary in character. And the souls, of course, do not stay put. They voyage, as the photographs of this book leave no doubt.

New Orleans' cemeteries are like New Orleans: they swing between destitution and opulence but always with style. Even the humblest marker in Potter's Field projects something native: the pathos of the scrawled names and the black-bordered cross rhymes with the willow and the mossy oak against the cloudy sky. The mightiest marble in the Metairie Cemetery says no more than this, though loudly instead of whispering. The dead in New Orleans are interred above the muddy gumbo of the soil to keep them from slipping away in the water. The dead are drier than the living, and that accounts for their air of superiority. They have shelter, eternity, and are cautiously but faithfully attended by the living. They are also more numerous than the living—New Orleans is an old city—and love to congregate, haunt, and dance. Only the thinnest film, a razor-edge of twilight, separates them from their descendants. The clouds in Sandra Russell Clark's views are no mere romantic props but portents and soul carriers. They drift over the graves, ghostly tour boats from which the dead view their own abodes as well as the living.

On All Saints' Day, the kin of the departed gather in cemeteries to clean the tombs, wipe off the grime of late twentieth-century air, brush away oak leaves, uproot impertinent banana trees, pick up cigarette butts and used syringes, and scrub clean the graffiti that, like a new force of nature, beset even the noblest. The keepers of the graves are mostly old women these days, who remember their *mamère* and *papère* and *gran'mère* and *gran'père*. Their own resting places wait for them in the family crypts. To make room, the oldest bones are lowered into a pit at the bottom. The recently dead are assured their berth until another generation displaces them. Great care is taken in planning which berth to lie on. Ending up next to a disliked relative can sour eternity. The grave keepers listen to the bones, remember, plot, pray, and scrub.

The city's first dead were, of course, the French and Spanish, a few of them nobles, who had the misfortune to settle in the fetid swamp from which New Orleans emerged. Later Europeans, notably non-noble Irish and German peasants, died of yellow fever and cholera. Some of the nobles perished young, and when their epitaphs include the word *honor*, it usually means they were killed in a duel. The scions of colonial nobility carried the manners of old Europe to their graves, but the occasion for the duels belonged wholly to the New World. At St. Louis Cemetery I, for instance, there is one Louis Philogene Duclos, whose stone proclaims, "Ci gît Louis Duclos, enseigne dans les Troupes des Etats Amérique, fils légitime de Rodolphe Joseph Duclos et de Marie Lucie de Reggi. Né le 18 août 1781, décédé le 4 juillet 1801." Louis died before the War of 1812, so it is not quite clear to which American troops he belonged, but one thing is very clear: the word *légitime* means that he was the result of a liaison between a French Creole and an octoroon mistress. We will never know if Louis was recognized before he died, but in the end he was brought into the bosom of the family. Creole men had quadroon and octoroon mistresses whose offspring were occasionally admitted to the family tomb, though never to the family table. The neighborhood where these women lived, in pretty cottages smothered in jasmine and screened by weeping willows, still stands. Their graves are less easily found. Louis' mother lies in anonymity, though one might easily imagine Louis' father defending her honor in a duel. The complexities of love, lust, honor, and skin color swirl in a fine mist around the gravestones of New Orleans.

Such mythic beginnings, still visible in the oldest cemeteries, like St. Louis I, translated into yet more extravagant complexities later. At the close of the last century and the beginning of this one, New Orleans became North America's pleasure dome. Out of its fleshpots exploded jazz, America's music. The institution of the mistress was reaffirmed, and some of the later mistresses were not to be trifled with even in death. Josie Arlington was a notorious *fille de joie* who carefully designed her tomb to tower over the more modest resting place of her married lover and his legitimate wife. Josie's image struck flambeaux on each side to project a rose light that made it seem as if she haunted the place. It is a sad fact that all flesh must die, but there is no reason one's story, any more than one's soul, should be slighted after the passage. The attraction artists feel for our cemeteries is only partly aesthetic; much of it has to do with gossip, a continual whisper intended for the delighted ear. Marble without a story is just marble. A true monument leans over and murmurs its secrets.

The graves of New Orleans follow social standing just as their occupants did. I have not looked rigorously into the distribution of angels, but I assume that the wealthy commissioned them. One time, marching past St. Roch Cemetery around twilight with a group of antifascist demonstrators, I was struck by the proliferation of angels massed in the sky. They were in flight, taking off toward one another, as animated as large winged creatures ever get. Their milky white flesh glowed, their robes came undone, the flowers they held glistened, their hair was on fire. The candidate against whom we were marching was defeated the next day. Miracles are very much part of St. Roch: look at the prosthetic limbs left behind by the faithful in the St. Roch chapel. The believers were healed—perhaps made strong enough to march for justice. Faith may have no politics, but it seems to belong disproportionately to the poor, which makes it fitting that the angels of the rich lent themselves to our cause.

The majority of the tombs of New Orleans are *sans anges*: they resemble baking ovens and are called burial ovens. The dead, laid out like bread loaves, seem to be baking quietly in the sun. Perhaps when they are as crisp as the baguettes at La Madeleine, they can leave their graves and frolic with the rest. "We bake in Purgatory," Dante said, "before we are set on the Table of Judgment, / sure to hear our story again."[1]

Some tombs are constructed out of the remnants of other tombs, whose owners have vanished. In 1866, the famous Theatre d'Orleans, which had diverted the Creoles for decades, burned down, and the owner of the Louisa Street Cemetery bought its bricks to build burial ovens.[2] To hear someone say, as I did, that New Orleans cemeteries "sing at night" is thus not altogether surprising. Of course they do, and that is why people sing even louder: to drown out the dead. Any given night on Rampart Street you can listen to the competition: the singers and bands making merry at The Funky Butt are barely heard above the din of dead choruses and howling cats across the street at St. Louis I.

New Orleans' cemeteries sing at night, but they are pretty quiet in the morning, when I take my coffee there. I started using places of eternal rest as my private coffeehouse way back in my teens, to get away from the horrible noise of adults. In my hometown of Sibiu, in Transylvania, Romania, there was a German Catholic cemetery that was as angel-rife and ornate as any in New Orleans. I wrote poetry among listing urns and reposing burghers and dreamt of the day when I would take a girl there to show her my favorite inscriptions. That day came soon enough, and I surrendered my virginity to our resident junior-high nymph, Marinella, on the grave of one Herr Titus Bruckenthal, a candlemaker, if memory serves right. When I moved to New Orleans, I was overjoyed to be living within walking distance of Lafayette Cemetery, which has a fair number of Germans baking in it. The Lafayette Cemetery also sits diagonally across from the apartment house where F. Scott Fitzgerald is rumored to have begun his first novel, *This Side of Paradise*. From his window, Scotty, possibly hung over on Prohibition gin, would have had a pretty good view of the tombs in the Lafayette. "All right," he may have addressed the entombed, "it ain't so hot on *this* side of Paradise."

I once went with the Polish artist Krystof to the Lafayette for a cup of coffee. Sitting on the funeral slab of a certain Tadeusz Millhauser, he told me about a student strike he had led in Warsaw during the late days of communism. He had taken his fellow students to the old Warsaw cemetery, and they had pieced together Polish historical truth from the tombstones, as a corrective to the lies in their propaganda textbooks. The dead in the Lafayette listened carefully, taking notes for their nightly meetings. I would not be surprised if Krystof's story became a song that traveled throughout the world of the dead and was instrumental in

1. Dante Alighieri, *The Divine Comedy*, my translation.
2. Herbert Asbury, *The French Quarter* (New York, 1938), 125.

12

bringing down the Berlin Wall a few weeks later. When I took Krystof across the street to Commander's Palace, we found the restaurant booked solid until I explained that my friend was Vaclav Havel, the future president of Czechoslovakia. The dead in New Orleans, in addition to singing, pay for the stories they hear by smoothing the way to restaurant tables.

A waiter at Antoine's, one of the city's grand restaurants, caused a problem by dying without designating a successor. A rabbi from New Jersey put it, "I lived in New Orleans for five years, and I finally got my own waiter at Antoine's. Then he died, and I moved. I had no idea how to get another waiter. Mine came to me from a blue-blood New Orleanian who bequeathed him to me when he had to move to Paris to take care of his dying sister." Waiting tables at Antoine's is itself a hereditary position, passed on from father to son. A true New Orleans blue blood must have a waiter as well as a tombstone, and a waiter must have a true blue-blood client as well as a tombstone. For myself, the pleasure of eating in an old restaurant is intimately linked to the comfort of death. Ah, I think to myself at Antoine's, or Commander's Palace, or any of the great establishments, one hundred years ago a man sat where I sit now, had a fine meal, and died. This makes me inexpressibly happy. I feel that my pleasure is authorized by continuity, that it is not ephemeral the way it is in those horrid spanking new, automobile-riddled, and soulless clusters that can pass for cities in America.

I have visited dead poets in famous cemeteries and found them at work. In the Protestant cemetery in Rome, John Keats lies under a tombstone that does not bear his name. "This grave contains all that was mortal of a YOUNG ENGLISH POET who on his death bed in the Bitterness of his Heart at the Malicious Power of his Enemies, Desired These Words to be Engraven on his Tombstone: Here Lies One Whose Name is Writ in Water. February 24th 1821." A lyre-shaped tree shadows the grave and shelters the cats of Rome, who love these grounds. Walt Whitman had his monument in Camden, New Jersey, placed in a circular grove of oaks. The tomb cost Whitman more than his house. On the grave of Guillaume Apollinaire, in the Père-Lachaise Cemetery, in Paris, there is a poem arranged in the shape of an inverted heart: MON COEUR PAREILLE À UNE FLAMME RENVERSÉE (My heart like an upside-down flame).

Tombstones are essential tools of poetry. I am speaking not only of the tombstones of poets, which are, of course, professional tools, but of all tombstones. New Orleans' cemeteries are among the most poetic I have ever visited.

They are a motherlode for poets, and I have taken my students to them on many an occasion. Cemeteries bring out the storyteller in people. My friend James Nolan, a New Orleans–born poet, who lived for many years in Spain and San Francisco, returned here and began writing stories about his family tomb. In New Orleans, he told me, the dead lead an active afterlife. They are invoked frequently, remembered often, and sometimes *seen*. More important, they speak to the living, and are not really shy about it.

The Voodoo religion, which is a mix of African worship and Catholic rite, takes the dead very seriously. Offerings are made at gravesites, and the dead are addressed with the greatest respect. The tomb of Marie Laveau, the so-called Voodoo Queen, who popularized these practices in the late nineteenth century, is often festooned with charred bones, half-empty glasses of rum, cigars that have been a little smoked, coins, feathers, and prayer-poems. In the French Quarter courtyard of one of my friends, a stone Voodoo shrine is mysteriously attended every full moon. The worshipers leave behind offerings, but my friend has never been able to see them, in spite of waiting and watching.

It is important to get to one's final resting place in vivid and memorable fashion. In New Orleans, the jazz funerals of important members of the black community are shining models of respect and remembrance. The deceased are seen off by musical bands, followed by dancing friends, acquaintances, and strangers. The throng sways under twirling yellow-and-black umbrellas, accompanying the deceased as near to the next world as is possible for the living. Surely, people who show their affection in this way have a friend in the next world. I once followed such a procession, without a clue as to whose funeral it was, and when we got to the cemetery, a man assured us, "You have one trumpet on your side when you go." It turned out the observance was for a trumpeter. I don't have my own waiter at Antoine's, but I have a trumpet in heaven.

Sandra Russell Clark views our Elysium from a double perspective. One is romantic, dramatic, and stormy and resembles that of Clarence John Laughlin, the poet and photographer who tried to make his camera penetrate the very veil of death. Clark does not have the same transcendental ambitions, but she photographs the statuary as if it holds an occult key. She is persuaded by the drama inherent in stone and weather. Laughlin sometimes dressed up funeraria with the bodies of the living, pushing the marble to speak his own romantic text. He staged the monuments to narrate a symbolist tale he directed. Clark lets the tombs tell their own story, but her view resembles Laughlin's in its faith that eternity—or at least the representation of it—is serious business. Though Laughlin let us see a wicked grin now and then, the afterlife was not funny to him. Clark is similarly possessed of an awe that nearly squares with the original intentions of her mortuary objects. The angels are always flying, the weather is always sultry. The view from this perspective is respectful and, in a Pre-Raphaelite sense, *beautiful*. One finds it hard to imagine these angels coming off their pedestals to smoke a cigarette.

But Clark's second perspective leads her also to view the mystery of forms without comment. Time scrambles the signs: what we see is the formal interaction of elements in which the original intentions can no longer be read. The passage of time fascinates her, and she photographs it as if it were the work of a great artist—which, of course, it is. Her subject is often the abstract content of Time's work, and from that she wrenches her melancholy and mysterious pictures.

The Seductive Face of Death

Patricia Brady

ALKER PERCY once wrote that New Orleans is "cut adrift not only from the South but from the rest of Louisiana, somewhat like Mont Saint-Michel awash at high tide." The French called their colonial city's site and its environs the Ile d'Orléans, the island of Orleans—an imaginary island moored between river and lake, its upper and lower boundaries stretching mistily off to bayous in the north and the Gulf in the south. When Napoleon sold this unwanted bit of real estate to the Americans—along with nearly a million acres as lagniappe—Yankee politicians found the city so foreign that they lobbied to give it back. Malls, chain stores, and fast-food outlets may have sprung up like toadstools in the twentieth century, but New Orleans still enchants with its exotic decadence and penchant for excess. It is a foreign island on the remotest fringe of the country, not completely American in culture or outlook even today.

Jazz, architecture, festivals, legal code, attitude toward life—everything in New Orleans has a different twist. But the city's way of death may be the most distinctive aspect of its distinctive culture. For more than two hundred years, New Orleanians have housed the departed in aboveground tombs, built along the streets and alleys of miniature cities of the dead, ghostly reflections of the city of the living. For all their Gallic feel, the oldest of these cemeteries dates back not to the

French colonial period but to the Spanish; all the rest were built after the Louisiana Purchase.

Officially founded in 1718, French New Orleans was laid out and occupied in 1721–1722, and very shortly afterward it was flattened by a hurricane. For the next forty years the impoverished colony struggled to survive, its meager population replenished from time to time by immigration—forced or voluntary—but almost as regularly reduced by death.

The city was excessively wet then, and it is excessively wet now. There is more water than land in south Louisiana, and the boundary between them shifts so imperceptibly that it's sometimes hard to tell which is which. On humid days, water and air lose precise definition, the air so languorous and heavy with water that pedestrians seem to swim through it. The site chosen for New Orleans—the present-day French Quarter—had a water table only a couple of feet beneath the soil. The land sloped back from the river toward Lake Pontchartrain, dropping rapidly below sea level. Rainwater, river seepage, floodwater—immense quantities of water drained into the moss-hung cypress swamps, the "drowned woods" of the French, in the amorphous area at the back of town.

Where in this wilderness of water were the colonists to bury their dead? The highest and driest area in town was along the banks of the Mississippi. There natural levees had been built up over the ages with soil deposited by the river's current. Logically enough in the very earliest days of the colony, the dead were interred in the riverbank. At high water, unfortunately, bodies washed out of their muddy graves and into the town's streets. Within the next couple of years, a graveyard was laid out beyond the municipal boundaries. At least there, if floods unearthed bodies, they were washed farther back into the swamps, decently out of sight. This first cemetery, overseen by the priests of the St. Louis parish church, was on the projected St. Peter Street in a square of ground bounded by what were to be Toulouse, Rampart, and Burgundy streets and reached by a winding dirt path from town.

Placing the cemetery at the farthest convenient reach for burial ceremonies was not just an aesthetic decision. It was commonly believed that graveyards and marshy ground, inextricably mingled in New Orleans, exuded a "miasma" of noxious vapors whose wraithlike embrace carried epidemic disease. The location outside town was considered a wise precaution against infection in a place already known for its high death rate.

Most burials in the St. Peter Street Cemetery were belowground; probably a few small brick tombs were above the surface. The wealthy and distinguished, as well as the clergy, however, enjoyed the privilege of being buried within the parish church or on its grounds. The cemetery, long since built over, was as shabby and ill kempt as the town it served until the end of the eighteenth century.

Ceded to Spain in 1762 to compensate for losses suffered as France's wartime ally, Louisiana was such a negligible prize that the Spanish waited years before sending officials to the colony, taking indisputable control only in 1769. Louisiana Creoles remained stubbornly and proudly French in culture and language during twenty years of prosperity and steady population growth under Spanish rule. New Orleans continued to bury its dead in the St. Peter Street Cemetery, whose grounds filled and grew rank at the same time that the city blocks near it were built up. Within an ordinary year or so, the city was going to need a new graveyard.

But 1787 and 1788 were far from ordinary years. They were years of calamities so terrible that it seemed as if the four horsemen of the Apocalypse, led by Death on his pale horse, had loosed fire, flood, and pestilence on New Orleans. Virulent smallpox—which had first made its deadly appearance in the city at the end of the previous decade—reappeared in 1787. Unusually malignant epidemics of malaria and influenza were right behind. As people by the hundreds died, the St. Peter Street Cemetery became perilously overcrowded, with moon-bleached bones sticking up through the earth.

The following year, fire broke out on Good Friday; driven hard by an unswerving southern wind, it swept through the city, destroying most of its houses, businesses, and public buildings, including the parish church of St. Louis. Easter Sunday's message of resurrection must have seemed grimly appropriate to people gagging at the stench of blackened, still-smoldering ruins. Just months after the city's devastation by fire, gusts of steadily rising wind from the Gulf proved to be the forerunners of a hurricane, whose high winds and heavy rain damaged buildings and flooded the city.

A new graveyard was desperately needed: the old cemetery was closed, its land eventually sold as building lots, and the first of the classic St. Louis cemeteries was officially opened in 1789. Besides this cemetery, all the other landmarks that define historic New Orleans were built after the catastrophes of 1787 and 1788, during the Spanish period. The only French colonial building still standing is the Ursuline Convent. The city's houses and businesses were rebuilt following a new code, mindful of fire, that called for brick construction and tile roofs. The now-familiar plastered and painted brick, the galleries and balconies, and the courtyards entered through arched carriageways show the influence of southern Spain and the West Indies. The new St. Louis Church—now St. Louis Cathedral—was completed in 1794, and the Cabildo in 1799. The Presbytère was begun in 1791 and halted in 1789; it acquired a second floor in 1813. The French Quarter today does not remotely resemble the original French colonial town.

The new St. Louis Cemetery was a walled enclosure with its main entrance on Rampart Street, just beyond the palisade erected to guard the town. The other boundaries were St. Louis, Tremé, and Conti streets. Oddly enough, given the French and Spanish penchant for laying out streets on a grid, the aisles of the new cemetery were a jumble, not a clear sight line among them. St. Louis I is charmingly irregular. In Lafcadio Hearn's words, "The tombs seem to jostle one another, the graveyard is a labyrinth in which one may easily lose oneself."

Only a few of the most prominent citizens and priests were buried in the new church. The poor continued to be buried in unmarked ground in the cemetery until the mid-nineteenth century. As the available space was filled with bodies, the level of the soil tended to sink. Contracts for dirt were frequently let, and city chain gangs shoveled it evenly over the surface, making room for another layer of bodies. Beneath the earth of today's cemetery, there must be bones several feet deep.

For everyone else, aboveground tombs became the rule. The practical reason is obvious: graves dug in the swampy ground of New Orleans immediately filled with water, and coffins floated forlornly on its muddy surface. Hefty gravediggers put heavy stones or gravel on the coffin lid, sometimes adding their own weight until the coffin sank and they could fill the grave with earth.

Early tombs were simple and functional rectangular enclosures of locally made soft red brick, plastered and whitewashed, with stepped tops or pitched roofs and the simplest of architectural decoration. After an interment, the opening to the tomb, its front door, so to speak, was bricked and sometimes plastered over. Many tombs were finished with marble enclosure tablets, expensive because the marble had to be imported.

During the Spanish period, tombs were the work of brickmasons, competent craftsmen but not artists. Many of the best masons in the city were free men of color, and the mason's trade today is dominated by their descendants. The same is true of the ironwork—wrought (not cast) iron crosses, tomb enclosures, and benches, throwing shadows of mortality across the pale walls of tombs.

The day when architects would design tombs in elaborate styles was a half century away. Nor were there sculptors in the city to memorialize sorrow in stone, even well into the territorial period. When the wife and daughter of Governor William C. C. Claiborne died, he had their tomb designed by an architect on the East Coast and the sculptured plaques rendered by an Italian artist. New Orleans was not yet a favored destination for itinerant artists; the only fine artist in the city was José Salazar, whose highly finished formal portraits of the colonial elite bring to life the figures who occupy the tombs.

American observers often noted with disapproval the lack of racial segregation in the cemetery. There was no separate "colored section" out back. The dead, after all, were no longer concerned with society's prejudices. But the cities of the dead, as Marcel Proust once wrote, say much less about the dead than about the living. St. Louis I reflected the laissez-faire attitude of New Orleans toward its large and successful population of free people of color. The races intermingled, if not quite freely, at least with much more ease than in any American city. Business and family relationships were recognized and accepted; the children of interracial liaisons were provided for, not denied. Black and white lived next door to each other in life and in death. In St. Louis I lie Etienne Boré, Bernard de Marigny, Charles Gayarré, Myra Clark Gaines, and Paul Morphy, with their neighbors Homer Plessy, Marie Laveau, Jean François Clay, and the mothers of Camille Thierry and Eugène Warburg.

For those who could not afford a private tomb but dreaded the soggy earth, there were two options: wall vaults and society tombs, both echoes of Spanish customs. The ranks of vaults, three or four high, built into the walls surrounding New Orleans cemeteries are one of the cemeteries' most striking features. With their arched openings, they resemble nothing so much as old-time bakers' ovens; people referred to them as *fours*, or ovens. Society tombs were the precursors of today's mausoleums. Burial societies constructed the tombs to offer their members relatively inexpensive interment. Such societies were generally organized by ethnic origin—Portuguese, Italian—but also grew out of other associations, such as the Orleans Battalion, veterans of the Battle of New Orleans.

With the Louisiana Purchase, in 1803, New Orleans came under the rule of the United States. Its economy started to boom, and by 1860 it was one of the nation's richest cities. Americans flooded the city, joined by merchants from all over the globe. The city's population doubled and redoubled, and the pleasant ways of Creole life came under the critical gaze of the newcomers.

Generally Protestant, American businessmen were hostile to the Catholic church and found the St. Louis Cemetery completely unlike their tidy churchyards back home and thus, of course, inferior. Even in a city with a severe land shortage, the efficient practice of reusing a tomb many times struck them as grossly offensive. After interment, the tomb could not be reopened for a year and a day, the time presumed sufficient by some for decomposition. When another family member needed a burial place, the earlier coffin was removed and broken up and the remains shoved to the back of the tomb into the *caveau*, or pit. In society tombs, the pit was in the center. The practical French saw no need to make a cult of the dead: a cemetery to them was simply a boneyard. Americans, reputedly so hard-headed and shrewd, were appalled. Sentimental views about the resurrection of the body inclined them to preservation.

By 1820, the city was outgrowing its boundaries, reaching Rampart Street, and the colonial cemetery was growing crowded. The city council looked for a new site farther out of town, close enough for funeral processions but far enough away to avoid contagion. They chose a long rectangle of land stretching from Canal Street (the cemetery no longer extends that far) to St. Louis Street, bounded by Claiborne and Robertson streets, and turned it over to the wardens of the cathedral. Burials began there in 1823.

St. Louis Cemetery II is laid out in a symmetrical grid with a straight center aisle and side aisles, divided into three squares. In other ways a continuation and elaboration of St. Louis I, Saint Louis II is the very embodiment of the idea of a city of the dead. Its well-built, large houselike tombs are as neatly arranged on their streets as the houses in any planned suburban community. Over time, the tombs became generally larger, grander, and more carefully planned than those in St. Louis I. The ironwork, too, is much more elaborate, with intricate cast iron elements mingled with the familiar wrought iron. Very large society tombs loom like skyscrapers. Belowground burials continued here as well, with contracts let for loads of soil to cover and press down the accumulation of bones.

St. Louis II also reflects social changes in New Orleans, as the city increasingly came under the influence of the racial prejudices of the American South. Unlike the first cemetery, St. Louis II was racially segregated. Square 3, between Iberville and Bienville streets, was set aside for black burials. Oscar J. Dunn, Henriette Delille, and Marie Couvent are buried there, separated from Pierre Soulé, François Xavier Martin, and Dominique You by a transparent wall of racism.

The church wardens planned ahead for the sickly season of late summer and early fall, contracting with builders for a few very simple tombs and banks of wall vaults in both St. Louis cemeteries in anticipation of epidemics. Among others, the cemetery sexton, the architectural and building firm of Gurlie and Guillot, and the young Florville Foy, a free man of color who was to become the proprietor of one of the city's most successful marble yards, built wall vaults at thirty-five dollars apiece, ten or twenty at a time, ensuring that sufficient burial places were available when needed.

There is no documentary evidence that trained marble cutters worked in New Orleans during the colonial period, and the simple tablets and tombs of that time are eloquent of their absence. But after the Louisiana Purchase, French marble cutters began to come to the booming city. Prosper Foy, a Napoleonic veteran, who seems to have been the first on the scene, in 1806, was followed by a number of his countrymen, among them Paul Monsseaux, the most accomplished of the early arrivals. Later in the century, very well trained Italian sculptors and marble cutters were attracted by the opportunities in the burgeoning graveyards—Achille Perelli the best of them. Few blacks were marble cutters or sculptors, but they dominated related jobs in the cemeteries—masonry, foundation and tomb erection, and marble setting. Florville Foy, Prosper's son, and Eugène and Daniel Warburg were very talented exceptions.

Jacques Nicolas Bussière de Pouilly, a French architect who landed in New Orleans in 1833, brought sophisticated tomb design to the city. With advanced academic training, de Pouilly designed tombs that show the influences of classical monuments and of the great Parisian cemetery Père-Lachaise, opened fifteen years after St. Louis I. His designs, as executed by local marble cutters, beautified New Orleans' cemeteries and encouraged others to attempt grander and more aesthetically ambitious tombs. Marble cutters who were also sculptors began to set standards of stylistic excellence in the execution of tombs. Cutters also turned their tools to funerary sculpture—plaques, bas-reliefs, and carved decorations.

St. Louis I and II are the archetypes of the classic New Orleans cemetery, but a number of other important cemeteries were opened in the nineteenth century, many of which are still functioning today. Catholicism was the religion of the majority of New Orleanians well into the twentieth century, but the influx of Protestants after the Louisiana Purchase and a growing Jewish community created a demand for cemeteries outside the control of the Church.

Christ Church (Episcopal), which had overseen burials in the Protestant section at the rear of St. Louis I since 1805, opened its own cemetery in an upriver suburb in 1822, and this served the Protestant community for more than a century. Always more utilitarian than grand, the Girod Street Cemetery was eventually eclipsed by more fashionable burial grounds. Neglected and sadly overgrown, it became an eyesore that was demolished and sold as building lots in 1957; most of its inhabitants were moved to Hope Mausoleum.

The Jewish cemeteries of Gates of Mercy, on Jackson Avenue, and Dispersed of Judah, on Canal Street, were the next to be built, in 1828 and 1946 respectively. Gates of Mercy has been demolished. The remaining historic Jewish cemeteries are Gates of Prayer, opened in 1850 uptown on Joseph Street; Gates of Prayer, opened in 1858 on Canal Street, and Hebrew Rest, opened in 1860 on Elysian Fields Avenue. All are relatively unimposing but well kept. The graves are generally marked with simple headstones, except for such grand memorials as those to the Haber and Levy families in Hebrew Rest. The cemeteries' air of simplicity reflects the Jewish belief that there is no afterlife—people live on in the memories of their families and friends—so elaborate funerary mansions are unnecessary.

Lafayette Cemeteries I and II, on Washington Avenue, are municipal cemeteries developed in the 1830s and 1850s in the city of Lafayette, now part of Uptown New Orleans. Lafayette I, with its white-painted brick walls and magnolia trees, has a peaceful, almost bucolic air; through the work of Save Our Cemeteries, an activist group founded some twenty years ago, it is the best-kept of the old cemeteries. It has been the setting for countless bad movies. The illicit use of St. Louis I in the culminating action of the classic sixties road film, *Easy Rider*, has made a cemetery scene de rigueur for any film shot in New Orleans, and the city makes Lafayette I easily available. Moviegoers who have never visited must have a bizarre picture of life in the city: attractive people sing out, "Let the good times roll," dance their way Uptown, catching a Mardi Gras parade and a jazz funeral on the way, to enjoy a midnight gunfight or car chase in Lafayette I. The neighbors are not amused.

Like Lafayette, the suburbs of Carrollton and Jefferson opened small municipal graveyards—the Carrollton and Valence Street Cemeteries. When the suburbs were incorporated into New Orleans, their cemeteries also came under the city's control. Both are quiet backwaters with unimpressive tombs.

Ever since the first appearance of yellow fever, in 1796, New Orleanians had dreaded its frequent outbreaks and high mortality rate. Acclimated natives seldom succumbed, but newcomers grew faint, feverish, and jaundiced, racked by the black vomit before they died. The last of the cathedral's burial places, St. Louis III, was opened on Esplanade Avenue in 1854, after the demise of thousands in the worst yellow fever epidemic in the history of New Orleans. Other Catholic cemeteries reflected new immigrant groups, like the largely Irish St. Patrick Cemeteries I and II. St. Roch Cemetery, honoring the saint who is said to shield his devotees against pestilence, was envisioned by a German priest. Dedicated in 1876, it includes a Gothic shrine where the faithful pray for recovery and leave votive offerings.

The secularization of cemeteries, generally as profit-making ventures, was an important nineteenth-century development. St. Vincent de Paul, for example, was owned by José Llula and then the Stewart family, now the proprietors of burial grounds worldwide. Benevolent associations such as the Odd Fellows, with their large membership and considerable economic clout, also went into the cemetery business.

The most spectacularly successful of the associations in the mortuary line was the Firemen's Charitable and Benevolent Association. For the benefit of firemen and their families, the association opened Cypress Grove in 1840, which it also made available to others. Tall gateposts and gatehouses, impressive memorials to fallen firemen, wide aisles, and shade trees signaled a radical change in the basic cemetery pattern followed in New Orleans for fifty years. It was so successful that the association opened Greenwood Cemetery in 1852.

If Cypress Grove and Greenwood were a departure from New Orleans traditions, the opulent Metairie Cemetery, organized by a group of businessmen and promoters and opened for burials in 1873, was the apotheosis of Victorian grandeur—and the ultimate antithesis to St. Louis I. It was heavily influenced by the great rural-park cemeteries created in the 1830s in the Northeast—Mount Auburn, in Cambridge, Massachusetts, Greenwood, in Brooklyn, and Laurel Hill, in Philadelphia. Those burial grounds, with their beautifully landscaped gardens, were major tourist attractions, and models for cemeteries around the country.

Metairie Cemetery, oval in shape because it was built on the grounds of a racetrack, was beautified with flowers and trees, lakes and bridges, and wide avenues and winding paths. Many tombs and sculptures there, as well as in Cypress Grove and in Greenwood, are on an almost Roman scale. Temples, pyramids, triumphal or broken columns, and monuments depicting Confederate generals, firemen, a ship's bell, and an elk—as well as the more expected pensive angels, lambs, and crosses of every possible sort—adorn the cemetery.

The older cemeteries shimmer palely white, with their whitewashed brick and white marble tombs. But the tombs of Metairie are polychrome fantasies. Polished marble and granite run the gamut of hues from white through red, brown, and black, and rough granite and limestone express the entire spectrum of gray, tan, and yellow tones.

The indigent dead for many years were buried in the grounds of the two St. Louis Cemeteries. The city council took over the responsibility of providing space for the interment of the poor with the nineteenth-century acquisition of the Locust Grove Cemeteries, on Freret Street. The city closed these cemeteries in 1879, however, and opened Holt Cemetery, on City Park Avenue, desirably situated farther out of town and on the higher ground of the Metairie Ridge. Live oaks grace the weedy, unkempt site, where a plot may be had by digging a grave. Markers are simple, usually homemade, and many plots are creatively decorated by families and friends. Lying in unmarked graves are many of the city's African American jazz pioneers, including Buddy Bolden. Holt, peacefully secluded, daydreams like a country graveyard.

New Orleans escaped the worst horrors of the urban renewal movement and the destructive expressways visited on most American cities. Despite major losses—the oak-shaded promenade of North Claiborne Avenue, the Robb house, the St. Charles Hotel—the city has retained a remarkable amount of its history in the French Quarter and its other old neighborhoods, as well as in its cemeteries.

Visiting the historic cemeteries is a stroll through the past of New Orleans. For many natives, cleaning and placing flowers on family tombs on All Saints' Day is still a hallowed tradition. The pain of losing several babies, the course of devastating epidemics—yellow fever, cholera, or Spanish influenza—waves of immigration, the nuances of social status, and a hundred other details of the city's life can be deciphered from the tombstones and enclosure tablets of the old cemeteries.

Collectively, they make up an invaluable archaeological site. In most cities, each successive century of urban life has been built atop earlier ruins, layer on layer deep in the earth. But in New Orleans, although much has been destroyed and covered by later construction, the many graveyards that have remained substantially intact provide access to the city's past.

Like the cemeteries, the older areas of town have suffered loss and deterioration, but their fragile charms—and many of their historic, if rundown, houses—have survived. Some people stayed put during the bad years, others have just moved back, but venerable neighborhoods are recapturing their character and atmosphere. Just so with the old graveyards: in the course of refurbishment and preservation, families are reusing their ancestral tombs, and abandoned sepulchers attract new owners. The cemeteries are fantastically implausible urban sculpture gardens. Their strange, decadent beauty is as seductive as New Orleans itself.

Elysium

a gathering of souls

NEW ORLEANS

. . . a dead bride crowned with orange flowers

. . . a dead face that asked for a kiss.

—LAFCADIO HEARN

St. Louis I

St. Louis I

St. Louis I

St. Louis I

St. Louis I

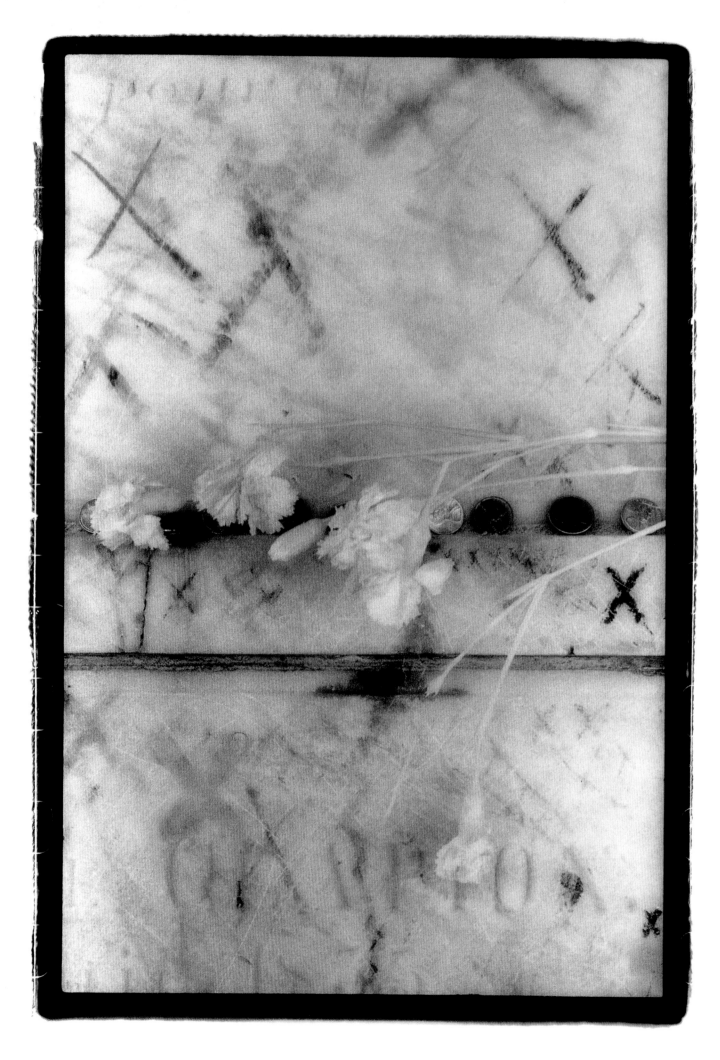

St. Louis I

The dead sleep a deeper sleep in their sepulcher

when offerings are there placed; . . . the ghosts of

departed friends accept such offerings as a token

that they are not wholly forgotten

St. Louis I

St. Louis I

St. Louis II

St. Louis II

I will build a chapel out of the astonished pain

And wait for bells ringing in an empty tower.

—ALLEN TATE

St. Louis II

St. Louis II

St. Louis II

St. Louis II

St. Louis II

St. Louis III

St. Louis III

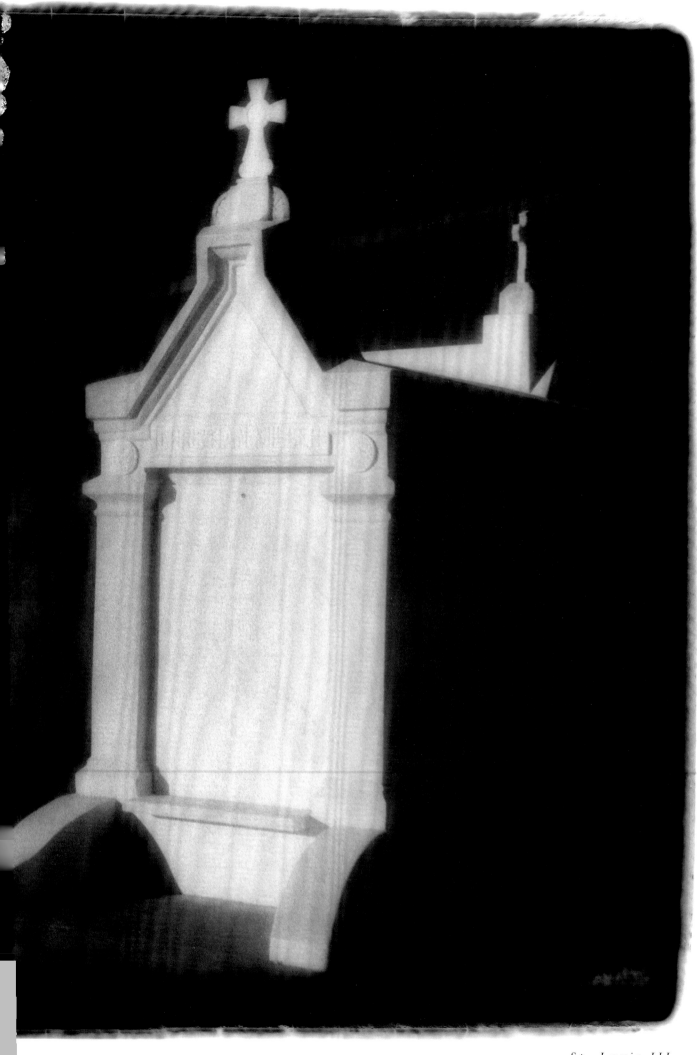

St. Louis III

St. Louis III

St. Louis III

St. Roch II

St. Roch I

Sometimes I go back, powerless as a Sunday afternoon

when shuttered sunlight casts its spell of powders

and I dream of saints' hands, boxes full of holiness,

lost for generations, marked fragile, expédite.

—JAMES NOLAN

St. Roch II

St. Roch I

St. Roch I

St. Vincent de Paul

Odd Fellows Rest

Odd Fellows Rest

Odd Fellows Rest

My sparrow, you are not here,

Waiting like a fern, making a spiny shadow.

The sides of wet stones cannot console me,

Nor the moss, wound with the last light.

—THEODORE ROETHKE

Odd Fellows Rest

Odd Fellows Rest

Odd Fellows Rest

Masonic

Only Time can hope to kill Memory and yet, like the Phoenix,

Memory rises again, passing from generation to generation,

the most valued of heirlooms.

—ELIZABETH ROSEN

Gates of Prayer I

Hebrew Rest

Hebrew Rest

Gates of Prayer II

Gates of Prayer II

Cypress Grove

Cypress Grove

Cypress Grove

Metairie

Yes, it is the exact location of the soul that I am after

. . . . It is elusive as the whippoorwill that one hears calling

incessantly from out the nightwindow, but which, nesting

as it does low in the brush, no one sees. No one

but the poet, for he sees what no one else can.

He was born with the eye for it.

— RICHARD SEEZER

Metairie

Metairie

Metairie

Metairie

Metairie

Metairie

Metairie

Metairie

Metairie

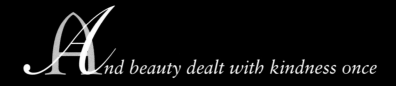

And beauty dealt with kindness once

And once the sky was tall, they say.

My flight lets fall a little dust.

My wings are on their mortal way.

—Raeburn Miller

Metairie

Metairie

Metairie

Metairie

Metairie

Sometime while night obscures the tree

The zenith of its life will be

Gone past forever, and from thence

A second history will commence.

—TENNESSEE WILLIAMS

Lafayette 1

Lafayette 1

Lafayette I

Lafayette I

Lafayette I

Lafayette I

Lafayette I

Carrollton

Valence Street

Carrollton

Carrollton

Words of heaven float over the broken stones,

The crosses leaning in the weeds, and mean

No more than a promise of clouds that might

Bring a moment's peace to this raw plot, before

The long parade of the living steps back

From the grief and the heat and the hollow ground.

—ELTON GLASER

Holt

Carrollton

Holt

Holt

Greenwood

St. Patrick I

St. Patrick I

Life is all memory, except for the one present moment

that goes by you so quick you hardly catch it going.

—TENNESSEE WILLIAMS

St. Patrick I

St. Patrick I

SACRED
to the memory of
CATHERINE LYON
of the parish of Call
Galway Ireland
who departed this life
December 2, 1859.

St. Patrick II

Greenwood

Greenwood

Greenwood

Greenwood

... *a garden of ghosts, a sunset*
world where twisting ivy
trickled down broken columns, where
arbors of spidersilk shrouded all.

—Truman Capote

Greenwood

Greenwood

Greenwood

Greenwood

St. Patrick II

Greenwood

Greenwood

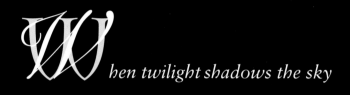 *hen twilight shadows the sky*

it is as if a soft bell were

tolling dismissal, for a

gloomy hush stills all, and

the busy voices fall silent

like birds at sunset.

—T RUMAN C APOTE

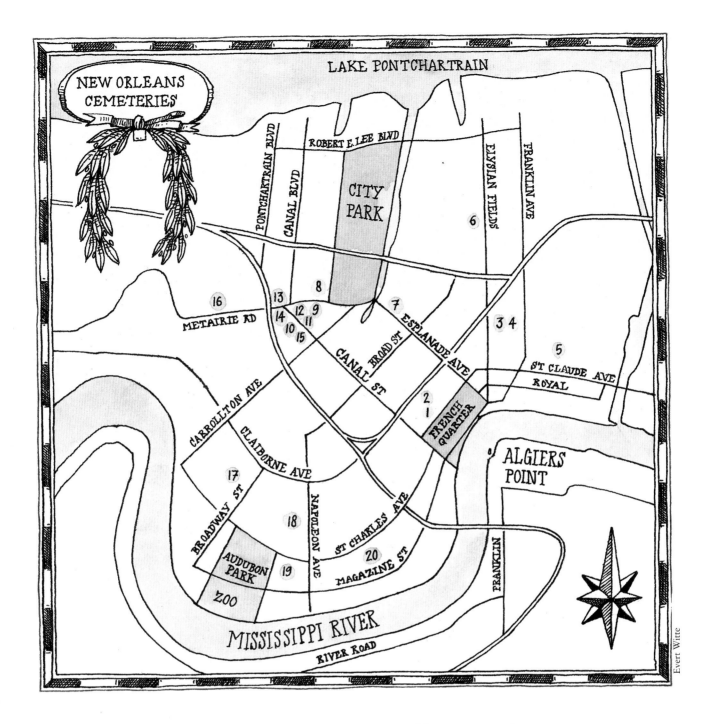

1. St. Louis Cemetery I

2. St. Louis Cemetery II

3, 4. St. Roch Cemeteries I and II

5. St. Vincent de Paul Cemetery

6. Hebrew Rest

7. St. Louis Cemetery III

8. Holt Cemetery

9. Masonic Cemetery

10, 11. St. Patrick Cemeteries I and II

12. Odd Fellows Rest

13. Greenwood Cemetery

14. Cypress Grove Cemetery

15. Gates of Prayer Cemetery I

16. Metairie Cemetery

17. Carrollton Cemetery

18. Valence Street Cemetery

19. Gates of Prayer Cemetery II

20. Lafayette Cemetery I

About the Cemeteries

PRESERVATION groups such as Louisiana Landmarks and the Preservation Resource Center have fiercely defended the endangered urban landscape of New Orleans, reclaiming it from demolition and neglect. Twenty years of community activism by Save Our Cemeteries, founded by Mary Louise Christovich, who also edited a well-known book on the city's cemeteries in the *New Orleans Architecture* series, has focused on saving the city's historic cemeteries. Without the preservationists' many victories, New Orleans would have been robbed of a vital part of its history.

New Orleans, like any large American city, has a crime problem, particularly in the older neighborhoods. Visitors to cemeteries should be cautious and alert, taking the same safety precautions they would in any similar urban setting. It is wise never to visit a cemetery alone.

1. St. Louis Cemetery I (1789). Basin and St. Louis streets, at the edge of the French Quarter. The oldest extant cemetery in the city, this has the same charm and historic interest as the Vieux Carre. It is on the National Register of Historic Places. Visit only with a tour group.

2. ST. LOUIS CEMETERY II (1823). Claiborne Avenue, between St. Louis and Iberville streets, Downtown. The second oldest extant burial ground in the city, this is the quintessential New Orleans cemetery, with a variety of tombs and fascinating occupants. It includes many tombs designed by the architect J. N. B. de Pouilly and is on the National Register of Historic Places. Extremely dangerous; visit only with a tour group that includes security.

3, 4. ST. ROCH CEMETERIES I (1874) and II (1895). 1725 St. Roch Avenue. Founded by a German priest, this campo santo with wall vaults and tombs is extremely picturesque. The Gothic chapel with votive offerings for favors granted is more characteristic of Latin America than the United States. Be careful here.

5. ST. VINCENT DE PAUL CEMETERY (*ca.* 1844). 1401 Louisa Street, Bywater. This was the first of the New Orleans cemeteries to be operated for profit rather than by a church. A few large tombs are surrounded by hundreds of smaller ones behind the brick wall and iron gates. Be very careful here.

6. HEBREW REST (1860–1861). Elysian Fields Avenue, between Senate and Pelopidas streets, Gentilly. The largest and most impressive of the Jewish cemeteries, this has interesting obelisks and large, well-designed tombs.

7. ST. LOUIS CEMETERY III (1854). 3421 Esplanade Avenue, Bayou St. John area. Very well kept, this has many fine tombs along its wide streets and aisles, which create a peaceful, uncluttered look. Maps of the cemetery are available at the office.

8. HOLT CEMETERY (1879). 635 City Park Avenue, alongside Delgado Community College. Shaded by live oaks, this potter's field is distinctive among the city's cemeteries. Although many graves are unmarked or overgrown with weeds, others are well-tended plots

decorated with works of naïve art. The neighborhood is quiet, but a high fence screening the cemetery from the street calls for caution.

9. MASONIC CEMETERY (1865). 400 City Park Avenue. The many tombs erected here by individual Masonic lodges capture the spirit of a fraternal order's cemetery.

10, 11. ST. PATRICK CEMETERIES I AND II (1841). 5000 Canal Street, 143 City Park Avenue. Founded by St. Patrick's Church to accommodate its many Irish immigrant parishioners, these are well-maintained cemeteries with some interesting tombs and statuary.

12. ODD FELLOWS REST (1849). 5055 Canal Street. This triangular burial ground, entered through cast iron gates with symbols of the organization, contains many society tombs. It is on the National Register of Historic Places.

13. GREENWOOD CEMETERY (1852). 115 City Park Avenue, corner of Canal Street and City Park Avenue. The second cemetery founded by the Firemen's Charitable and Benevolent Association, this features an impressive entrance and, on its wide lawns, memorials to firemen and Elks. Most of the cemetery, however, with sidewalks, streets, and rows of identical closely packed tombs, resembles a suburb of the dead.

14. CYPRESS GROVE CEMETERY (1840). 124 City Park Avenue. With its entrance flanked my impressive pylons and lodges and the large firemen's memorials at the front, this at first resembles Greenwood. But the large magnolias and firs and interesting tombs, some designed by de Pouilly, make the grounds unusually lovely.

15. GATES OF PRAYER CEMETERY I (1858). 4800 Canal Street. The belowground graves are marked with neat and generally modest headstones. A memorial in the form of a lighthouse is an exception.

16. METAIRIE CEMETERY (1873). 5100 Pontchartrain Boulevard, Metairie. With a lush parklike setting, huge architecturally designed tombs, and statuary, this is the most opulent cemetery of New Orleans. Its curving avenues follows the shape of the racetrack on which it was built. It is on the National Register of Historic Places.

17. CARROLLTON CEMETERY (1849). Adams Street, between Hickory and Birch streets, Carrollton. Originally a suburban cemetery, primarily for German and Irish immigrants, this was acquired by the city of New Orleans when it absorbed Carrollton. There are tombs as well as a potter's field.

18. VALENCE STREET CEMETERY (*ca.* 1860s). Valence Street, between Danneel and Saratoga streets, Uptown. A suburban cemetery, this was acquired by the city with the absorption of the city of Jefferson. There are several society tombs.

19. GATES OF PRAYER CEMETERY II (1850). Joseph Street, between Pitt and Garfield streets, Uptown. This Jewish cemetery was built when the area was in the city of Lafayette. Its neat tombs are surrounded by an iron fence.

20. LAFAYETTE CEMETERY I (1830s). 1400 block, Washington Avenue, Garden District. A suburban cemetery, this was acquired by the city of New Orleans with the absorption of the city of Lafayette. This is the safest and best kept of the traditional cemeteries, largely through the efforts of Save Our Cemeteries. It has very attractive magnolia trees and interesting tombs. It is on the National Register of Historic Places. Tours are available.

Acknowledgments

A very special thank-you to my husband, Evert Witte, for his unending patience, humor, and enthusiasm, and for the love he has given me throughout this project. Also, thanks to my family, friends, and patrons for their support these many years, and to the following for their contributions, talent, advice, and encouragement: Patricia Brady, Elizabeth Calvit of Save Our Cemeteries, Hiro Clark of Welcome Enterprises, Jan Clifford, Andrei Codrescu, Philippe Creplet, David Crumrine, Frank de Caro, Joseph DeSalvo and Joanne Sealy of Faulkner House Books, Beth Dickerson, Michael Eldred, Candice Everett, David Hanson of *Louisiana Literature*, Billy Henry, Janice Moore, James Nolan, Greg Osborne, Bill Rosen, Elizabeth Rosen, Adelaide Russo, Ruth Santer, Michael Sartisky of the Louisiana Endowment for the Humanities, Richard Sexton, Amy Weiskopf, Steve Winn, Harry Zimmerman, and all the writers whose passages accompany the photographs.

I would also like to thank John Easterly, Amanda McDonald Key, Barry Blose, and the staff at Louisiana State University Press for their guidance and their enthusiasm for this project. I am also grateful to the administrators of the cemeteries and the families whose tombs appear in *Elysium*.

St. Louis I

BIOGRAPHIES

SANDRA RUSSELL CLARK, a native of New Orleans, began photographing in 1978. She was director of photographic exhibitions at the Contemporary Arts Center, in New Orleans, from 1980 to 1985 and taught photography at Loyola University in the early 1990s. Her work was included in the Torino Fotografia Biennale Internationale in 1989 and was shown at the Museu da Imagem e do Som, in São Paulo, in 1993. It was also part of the 1991 exhibition *BilderLust,* which traveled to museums throughout Germany. Clark's photographs are in the New Orleans Museum of Art; the Museum of Fine Arts, in Houston; the Memphis Brooks Museum, in Memphis; the Guild Hall Museum, in East Hampton, N.Y.; the Uwescheid Collection, in Germany; and many private and corporate collections in the United States and abroad. Her work has appeared in magazines as well, among them *American Artist, Mirabella, The Traveler,* and *Vogue.*

ANDREI CODRESCU, who was born in Sibiu, Romania, emigrated to the United States in 1966. He has published poetry, fiction, memoirs, and essays and is a regular commentator on National Public Radio. He has written and starred in the Peabody Award–winning movie *Road Scholar.* His novel *The Blood Countess* was a national best seller. He teaches writing at Louisiana State University and edits the journal *Exquisite Corpse.*

PATRICIA BRADY, director of publications at the Historic New Orleans Collection, discovered New Orleans' cemeteries as a student at Newcomb College. A social and cultural historian, she has edited *Nelly Custis Lewis's Housekeeping Book; George Washington's Beautiful Nelly: The Letters of Eleanor Parke Custis Lewis to Elizabeth Bordley Gibson, 1794–1851; The Encyclopedia of New Orleans Artists, 1718–1918; Haunter of Ruins: The Photography of Clarence John Laughlin;* and *Arts and Entertainment in Louisiana.* She has contributed to a number of volumes and periodicals. Brady is vice-president for programming of the Tennessee Williams/New Orleans Literary Festival and past president of the New Orleans/Gulf South Bookseller Association. She is writing a book about free people of color in New Orleans.

Quotation Sources

Truman Capote, *Other Voices, Other Rooms*

William Faulkner, *As I Lay Dying*

Elton Glaser, "Black Baptist Funeral"

Lafcadio Hearn, *Letters from the Raven: Being the Correspondence of Lafcadio Hearn with Henry Watkin* and *Occidental Gleanings*

Raeburn Miller, "A Resurrection"

James Nolan, "The Invention of Hands on Columbus Street"

Theodore Roethke, "Elegy for Jane"

Richard Selzer, *Mortal Lessons: Notes on the Art of Surgery*

Allen Tate, "Ode to the Confederate Dead" and "The Progress of Œnia"

Tennessee Williams, *The Night of the Iguana*